October Journal Jumpstarts

A Month of Creative Writing Prompts

Written by
Cindy Barden

Editors: Barbara G. Hoffman and Michael Batty

Cover and Interior Design: Good Neighbor Press, Inc.

Illustrator: Chris Nye

FS112131 October Journal Jumpstarts

All rights reserved—Printed in the U.S.A.
23740 Hawthorne Boulevard
Torrance, CA 90505-5927

Notice! Pages may be reproduced for classroom or home use only, not for commercial resale. No part of this publication may be reproduced for storage in a retrieval system or transmitted in any form or by any means—electronic, mechanical, recording, etc.—without the prior permission of the publisher. Reproduction of these materials for an entire school or school system is strictly prohibited.

Copyright © 2000 Frank Schaffer Publications, Inc.

Table of Contents
October

Introduction	1
Thoroughly Thursday	2
When I Grow Up	3
Refugee	4
You Need to Know This	5
Snakes, Turtles, Alligators, and Iguanas	6
Sad	7
Sports	8
No Meanies Allowed!	9
What's for Lunch?	10
Look from the Other Side	11
My Perfect Day	12
Columbus Day	13
My Personal Logo	14
Making Choices	15
Oops	16
Happy Thoughts	17
Sunshine	18
Spread Happiness	19
Important Thing	20
Worry	21
Yellow	22
Favorite School Subject	23
I Think I Can	24
Something Nice	25
Teacher's Best	26
Games	27
A Statue for My Community	28
For the Better	29
October 31	30

Introduction

An empty journal is filled with infinite possibilities.

Writing regularly in a journal helps us to develop our imaginations, encourages us to express our thoughts, feelings, and dreams, and provides a way to communicate experiences in words and pictures. Many students feel frustrated when asked to keep a journal. They may not be sure of what to write, or they may be intimidated by a blank sheet of paper. Even professional writers occasionally face "writer's block." The Journal Jumpstarts series provides ideas and suggestions for daily journal entries. Each book contains 29 jumpstarts. You could give each student a photocopy of the same page or provide a variety of pages and allow students to choose their own topics. You may have students who will be able to sit and write without jumpstarts. At times students may prefer to express their thoughts through drawings or with a combination of drawings and writing. Be encouraging!

Through making regular entries in journals, students become more observant of themselves and the world around them. Journal writing on a regular basis strengthens students' attention spans and abilities to focus. Keeping journals promotes self-esteem because students are doing something for themselves—not for grades or in competition with others. A journal can become an essential friend, a confidante in times of personal crisis.

Encourage students to get into the journal habit by setting aside writing time every day at about the same time, such as first thing in the morning or shortly before lunch. Share their journal time by writing in your own journal. What better way to encourage a good habit than by example!

Note: Assure students that what they write is confidential. Provide a safe, secure place for students to store their journals. Respect their privacy, as you would expect your privacy to be respected—read their journals by invitation only.

Name _____ Date _____

Refugee

Pretend that you are a refugee from a war, on the road, and can't go home again. Write a letter to your teacher.

_____
_____
_____
_____

Name _____   Date _____

You Need to Know This

If a new student came to school tomorrow, write what he or she would need to know about your school, your class, and your teacher.

_____
_____
_____
_____
_____
_____
_____
_____
_____
_____
_____
_____
_____

Name _____ Date _____

Snakes, Turtles, Alligators, and Iguanas

If you could be a kind of reptile, which kind would you be? Describe what you think it would be like to be that kind of reptile.

_____
_____
_____
_____
_____
_____
_____
_____
_____
_____
_____
_____
_____
_____
_____
_____
_____

Name _____ Date _____

Sad

Write about something in a book or movie that made you feel sad. What happened? Why did it make you feel sad?

_____

_____

_____

_____

_____

_____

_____

_____

_____

_____

_____

_____

_____

FS112131 October Journal Jumpstarts   © Frank Schaffer Publications, Inc.
reproducible

Name _____ Date _____

Sports

Write about a sport that you like or dislike and tell why you feel that way about it.

Name _____   Date _____

No Meanies Allowed!

Write about how you feel when someone is mean to you. Then write what you can do to get that person to stop treating you badly.

_____
_____
_____
_____
_____
_____
_____
_____
_____
_____
_____
_____
_____
_____
_____
_____
_____

Name _____   Date _____

What's for Lunch?

Describe the tastes, textures, and smells of the foods that you'd eat if you could have anything that you'd like for lunch today.

_____
_____
_____
_____
_____
_____
_____
_____
_____
_____
_____
_____
_____
_____
_____
_____
_____
_____

© Frank Schaffer Publications, Inc.

reproducible

FS112131 October Journal Jumpstarts

Name _____ Date _____

Look from the Other Side

Write about a time when you disagreed with someone in your family, a teacher, or a friend. Then, pretend that you are the person with whom you disagreed and write what happened from his or her point of view.

Name _____ Date _____

My Perfect Day

Describe your idea of a perfect day. What would happen that would make it perfect?

_____
_____
_____
_____
_____
_____
_____
_____
_____
_____
_____
_____
_____
_____
_____
_____
_____
_____

© Frank Schaffer Publications, Inc. FS112131 October Journal Jumpstarts

Name _____ Date _____

Columbus Day

Christopher Columbus and his crew set sail on a voyage across unknown waters that would take an unknown amount of time. Pretend that you are Columbus and that you have been at sea for two months. All you've seen is sea, sky, and sea animals, and your crew is scared. Write about what you are thinking.

_____
_____
_____
_____
_____
_____
_____
_____
_____
_____
_____
_____

Name _____ Date _____

My Personal Logo

Imagine that you are about to become famous for inventing a new product. You want your product to be recognized easily, so you want to put your name on it in a special kind of design called a logo. Describe or draw a logo using your name. Use the back of this paper for your drawing.

Name _____ Date _____

Making Choices

Do your friends ever want you to do things that you think are bad or wrong? Write what you do or say when that happens.

Name _____   Date _____

Oops

Have you ever said something mean or told a lie and then felt bad about it? Write about why you felt bad and what you did or could have done to make things better.

_____
_____
_____
_____
_____
_____
_____
_____
_____
_____
_____
_____
_____
_____
_____
_____
_____
_____

Name _____ Date _____

Happy Thoughts

When Peter Pan taught Wendy and her brothers to fly, he told them to "think happy thoughts." Write some of your happy thoughts.

Name _____ Date _____

Sunshine

When you see sunshine, what does it make you want to do? Write about something that you did just because the sun was shining and describe how the sunlight made it more special.

_____

_____
_____
_____
_____
_____
_____
_____
_____
_____
_____
_____
_____
_____

© Frank Schaffer Publications, Inc. FS112131 October Journal Jumpstarts

Name _____ Date _____

Spread Happiness

Write about what you could do today to make someone happy. Then do it.

_____
_____
_____
_____
_____
_____
_____
_____
_____
_____
_____
_____
_____
_____
_____
_____

Name _____   Date _____

Important Thing

You have learned many things. Write about an important thing that you have learned. Describe why it is important to you.

Name _____ Date _____

Worry

What kinds of things do you worry about? Write about them and what you could do to make yourself feel better.

_____
_____
_____
_____
_____
_____
_____
_____
_____
_____
_____
_____
_____
_____
_____
_____
_____
_____

Name _____ Date _____

Yellow

There are many different shades of yellow. Write the names of some things that are yellow. Are all the things that you named the same shade of yellow?

Write about how you feel when you see something bright yellow and when you see something soft, light yellow.

_____
_____
_____
_____
_____
_____
_____
_____
_____
_____
_____
_____
_____
_____

Name _____ Date _____

Favorite School Subject

Write about your favorite subject in school. What do you like about it? Describe your favorite things to do while you are learning the subject, such as projects or activities.

_____
_____
_____
_____
_____
_____
_____
_____
_____
_____
_____
_____
_____
_____
_____
_____
_____

Name _____ Date _____

I Think I Can

Doesn't it feel great when you accomplish something that was difficult? Write about something hard that you did and how you felt before and after you did it.

_____
_____
_____
_____
_____
_____
_____
_____
_____
_____
_____
_____
_____
_____
_____
_____
_____

Name _____ Date _____

Something Nice

If you had all the money you needed to do anything you wanted, what would you do for someone that you live with? Write three things.

_____
_____
_____

_____
_____
_____
_____
_____
_____
_____
_____
_____
_____
_____
_____

Name _____ Date _____

A Statue for My Community

If you could design a statue for your school or community, what would it look like? Describe its size, shape, and color and where you would put it. Write the words that would be on it, if any.

_____
_____
_____
_____
_____
_____
_____
_____
_____
_____
_____
_____
_____
_____
_____
_____

Name _____ Date _____

For the Better

Write about things that would make your community a better place to live.

_____
_____
_____
_____
_____
_____
_____
_____
_____
_____
_____
_____
_____
_____
_____
_____
_____

Name _____   Date _____

October 31

Write about some of the things that you would like to do on the last day of October.